Long, long ago in the bloom of my youth,
I spoke with the Lord and He taught me His truth,
He offered to help me and serve as my guide,
He promised forever He'd walk by my side.

I trusted the Lord and obeyed His command,
And together we've walked through the years hand in hand;
But I recently had quite a curious dream:
I dreamed I was out on a beach by a stream;

I spotted some footprints etched deep in the sand
Arranged in a pattern as if they'd been planned;
And somehow I knew that those prints were my own-
And there was the proof I had not walked alone!

There were two sets of prints in a matching design,
The second set merging to parallel mine-
Except . . . for one stretch . . . there was only one pair-
The parallel footprints no longer were there!

Those days, I recalled, were the worst of my life,
I was burdened with cares and surrounded by strife;
So I said to the Lord, "I do not understand
That break in the footprints I see in the sand.

"It was then that I stumbled and strayed from my post
And that was the time when I needed You most."
The Lord sweetly smiled as He said, "That is true . . .
And that was the time I was carrying you."

by John T. Baker, Copyright 1999

Grant Me My Final Wish

Grant Me My Final Wish

A personal journal to simplify life's inevitable journey

by Renata Marie Vestevich

Bella Vita Books LLC

Grant Me My Final Wish: A personal journal to simplify life's inevitable journey.

The contents of this book are not intended as legal, financial or medical advice. To answer such issues, a qualified professional should be consulted.
Second printing 2008

ISBN: 0-9766382-0-7

LCCN: 2005902485

Cover Photography © by M. Timothy O'Keefe
Graphic Design by Jaime Lynn Pescia
Edited by Sharon R. Gunton

For information about special discounts
on quantity purchases, please contact:

Bella Vita Books, LLC
1265 Water Cliff Drive
Bloomfield Hills, MI 48302
1-800-589-0039
info@bellavitabooks.com
www.bellavitabooks.com

Dedication

I dedicate this book with love to:

My father, who is no longer with me,
but lives in my heart each and every day.

My mother, whose struggle to raise six children
after the death of my father has taught me the
true meaning of strength and sacrifice.

My brothers and sisters, for their continuing
unconditional love and friendship.

My nieces and nephews, for helping me once
again to see the world through children's eyes.

My husband, who is always encouraging me
to be myself and loving me just as I am.

My editor, Sharon Gunton, for her insight, care and
masterful editing. Her guidance, support and friendship
are true gifts in my life.

My graphic designer, Jaime Pescia, whose artistic talent
has greatly enriched my book.

The many others, who have each in their special way made
a contribution to this book. I am deeply grateful.

Contents

A Message from the Author

For each of us, life is a unique and wonderful journey. As we travel on this journey, we experience love, we gather memories, learn lessons, and obtain greater wisdom, which ultimately defines our very own, one-of-a-kind presence in this world.

But along with experiencing life, we also recognize the reality that our life will end. Death is never an easy topic to confront; consequently, planning proactively for one's own passing is almost unheard of. Many of the tasks and decisions that are carried out by loved ones when death occurs are drenched in pain and grief, but a number of the related details could have been outlined in advance, when heads were clear and hearts unburdened.

The tragedy of my family losses and my professional experiences have inspired me to create this journal. The sudden death of my father was the most profound, emotional ordeal I have endured. I was a typical 17-year-old high school senior, whose days were filled with homework, band practice, tennis and fun. The thought of death rarely entered my mind. I couldn't even imagine losing a parent or sibling. At the time, it never seemed possible.

My father suffered a massive heart attack, leaving behind his 39-year-old wife and six children. Within hours after his death, we had to face many difficult choices and plan for his funeral. My heart kept telling me this was all a terrible mistake, while my mind kept reminding me of the truth as we proceeded to make dozens of urgent decisions.

After the funeral, we were confronted with many legal and financial matters. Having to make these unexpected decisions during this time of intense grief was incredibly painful and difficult – almost too much to bear. This would not be the only traumatic loss I would have to endure.

Years later, my dear sister-in-law was diagnosed with leukemia at age 33. Her fighting spirit persevered for almost a year, before she lost her courageous battle against cancer. Prior to her death, our relationship deepened and our time together was spent talking about anything and everything – except death. During one of our final visits together, I sat next to her, holding her hand, sharing silent companionship. Although uncertain about this matter, I felt compelled to ask her if she cared to share her thoughts with me about dying. I remember how she struggled to sit up in her bed, began crying and thanked me for asking. She spoke for hours sharing her deepest fears, regrets and disappointments in life. She confided specific wishes that she would like to have honored upon her death. Several days later, she passed away peacefully.

Losing a loved one is certainly one of life's most heartbreaking experiences. The loss of those dear to me has taught me a great deal about love, life and death. I have learned to love unconditionally, live with a greater sense of appreciation for every experience I encounter, and to be less afraid, especially of death. I've learned that our fears don't stop death – they merely inhibit us from living a more complete life. Both my family losses and my professional involvement working with cancer patients have taught me the importance of planning for death. Nothing on this earth is as natural as the miracle of birth or the certainty of death. Instinctively, we are all aware of this fact, and yet, most of us are reluctant to totally and freely accept the natural balance of our existence. Many of our day-to-day activities are directed at making the most of what life has to offer; consequently, we seem to give little thought to the ending of life.

I encourage you to take control of an essential part of your life as you use this journal to organize and record important data and personally communicate your final wishes to your loved ones. And, it is my hope that *Grant Me My Final Wish* will help you celebrate your life and approach its end with peace of mind so that, ultimately, saying good-bye will be easier for you and those you leave behind.

Many Blessings,

Renata Marie

Introduction

Grant Me My Final Wish is a unique journal. Thoughtfully and compassionately written, it addresses important personal planning issues, questions and answers that need to be examined by everyone. For no matter how well we live our lives, we will eventually leave our family and friends behind.

Grant Me My Final Wish gives you the opportunity to thoroughly discuss and plan for life's inevitable journey by:

~ Organizing topics for your consideration and offering you a structured format for documenting important data

~ Helping you define specific requests you wish to be carried out at the end of your life, making it easier to express them to your loved ones or draw up a will or an ethical will

~ Giving you the reassurance that your important final wishes have been recorded, which will bring you and your loved ones a profound sense of comfort and peace of mind

Grant Me My Final Wish also gives you the opportunity to acknowledge the important influences and people in your life. It is a place to include favorite photographs and preserve your thoughts for family and friends. You can share all that truly matters to *you* – a chance to tell *your* story as only you can.

After expressing your wishes and sentiments in your journal, present a copy to the significant people in your life. It can serve as a cherished keepsake that will remain with your loved ones for generations.

A Special Gift

_____

presented to

_____

from

_____

date

A Personal Message from Me to You

My Personal Information

Full Given Name

Date of Birth

Place of Birth

Mother's Full Name

Mother's Date & Place of Birth

Father's Full Name

Father's Date & Place of Birth

Paternal Grandparents' Names

Dates & Places of Their Births

Maternal Grandparents' Names

Dates & Places of Their Births

Names of My Siblings

Dates & Places of Their Births

Spouse

Date & Place of Marriage

Children's Names & Birthdates

My Favorite Things

Color

Food

Book/Author

Movie

Song/Artist

Quote or Scripture

Sport/Sports Team

Flower

Perfume

Vacation Spot

Dessert

My Interests & Hobbies

*Let your thoughts be positive
for they will become your words.*

*Let your words be positive
for they will become your actions.*

*Let your actions be positive
for they will become your values.*

*Let your values be positive
for they will become your destiny.*

~ Mahatma Gandhi

Special Medical Wishes

Advance Directives

Living Will

Durable Power of Attorney for Health Care

Hospital Considerations

Organ and Tissue Donation

Hospice/Home Care

"Dear Lord, be good to me...
The sea is so wide and my boat is so small."
~Irish Fisherman's Prayer

Special Medical Wishes

We value human life, so the decisions to prolong life or end it are never easy. Imagine your family pressured to make that choice for you. No one wants to struggle with that decision. No matter what they decide, they will constantly wrestle with the thought: Did I make the right choice? The burden may be much easier to bear if you make your wishes clear to your loved ones.

What is important to you in life? What limitations or conditions would make your life no longer meaningful? Your answers may help you decide what future medical care you may receive.

Other questions you may want to consider:
What if I could no longer:
• care for myself without being a burden to others?
• go out on my own?
• make decisions for myself?
• participate in activities with my family and friends?
• live without being dependent on medical treatment or machines to keep me alive?

Expressing your medical wishes is important for everyone, young or old, since serious accidents and illness can strike at any age. Knowing that your wishes will be followed if you are unable to express them can bring you much peace of mind.

In addition to stating your medical wishes in your journal, consider the benefits of recording your wishes clearly in a Living Will and/or designating a Durable Power of Attorney for Health Care Decisions.

Advance Directives

Living Will   ☐ Yes   ☐ No

Date of Last Revision _____

Location of Documents _____

_____

Durable Power of Attorney for Health Care or Health Care Proxy

☐ Yes   ☐ No

Date of Last Revision _____

Location of Documents _____

_____

Name of person(s) appointed to make health care decisions if you are
unable to do so for any reason

Name _____ Relationship _____

Telephone _____

Name _____ Relationship _____

Telephone _____

Name _____ Relationship _____

Telephone _____

Hospital Considerations

Decisions pertaining to extraordinary methods to prolong life

Some of your treatment options include:

Cardio Pulmonary Resuscitations (CPR)

Ventilator Support

Kidney Dialysis - cleans your body when your kidneys no longer work

Tube Feedings

I.V. Fluids to provide nutrition and hydration

Pain Medication and other treatments to keep you comfortable

_____

_____

_____

_____

_____

_____

_____

_____

_____

_____

_____

Organ and Tissue Donation

Organ and Tissue Donation   ☐ Yes   ☐ No

I would like to make an Anatomical Gift effective on my death

              ☐ All organs

              ☐ All tissues (bone, eyes, other)

              ☐ Specific organs

Signature

Witness

Emergency Contact

Telephone

Additional Comments

Hospice and/or Home Health Care

Special Wishes

Gift - Rapt

Share the gift of courage,
And it may lead to forgiveness.
Share the gift of forgiveness,
And it may lead to hope.
Share the gift of hope,
And it may lead to peace.
This year, and every day,
Let us share gifts of the heart,
Which grow from a belief in
Something greater than us -
That which was before us,
That which is with us,
That which will be beyond us.
Let us think gently,
Speak gently,
Live gently...
And the world may be
Blessed gently
With the greatest gift of all...
Faith.

Important People to Notify

Employer

Physicians and Dentist

Funeral Director

Clergy

Attorney

Executor

Accountant

Financial Advisor

Insurance Agent

Professional and Social Affiliations

*"If the only prayer you ever say
in your whole life is 'thank you,'
that would suffice."
~ Meister Eckhart*

Important People to Notify

There are many important professional people who will need to be notified upon your death.

Use this segment of your journal as a guide to list those important people and provide contact information for your loved ones.

Employer

Name of Employer

Name of Contact Person

Telephone

Physicians

Name of Physician

Specialty

Address

Telephone

Name of Physician

Specialty

Address

Telephone

Name of Physician

Specialty

Address

Telephone

Name of Physician _____

Specialty _____

Address _____

Telephone _____

Name of Physician _____

Specialty _____

Address _____

Telephone _____

Name of Physician _____

Specialty _____

Address _____

Telephone _____

Dentist

Name _____

Address _____

Telephone _____

Funeral Director

Name

Address

Telephone

Clergy

Name

Address

Telephone

Attorney

Name

Address

Telephone

(Remember to have your Estate Plan Documents up-to-date and in a secure location.)

Executor

Name

Address

Telephone

Accountant

Name

Address

Telephone

Financial Advisor

Name

Address

Telephone

Stock Broker

Name

Address

Telephone

Insurance Agent

Name

Address

Telephone

Veterans Administration

Location of Discharge Papers

Telephone

Voters Registration Office

Location

Telephone

Professional and Social Affiliations
Fraternities

Name of Organization

Telephone   Website

Name of Organization

Telephone   Website

Sororities

Name of Organization

Telephone   Website

Name of Organization

Telephone   Website

Alumni Association

Name of Organization

Telephone

Health Club

Name of Health Club

Telephone

Other Social Affiliations

Name

Telephone

Name

Telephone

Name

Telephone

Name

Telephone

Additional Comments

Family and Friends to Contact

"To the world you may be one person
but to one person you may be the world."
~Anonymous

Family and Friends to Contact

One can't ever be prepared for the intense feelings that will overcome you when you have suffered a great personal loss. Notifying family and friends of a death is never easy. There are times when death comes without warning and without advance preparations.

Use the following pages to list family and friends you wish to notify. Providing this information for your loved ones will lessen their anxiety and uncertainty about knowing who should be contacted.

Name

Address

Home Phone   Work Phone

Mobile Phone   E-mail

Name

Address

Home Phone   Work Phone

Mobile Phone   E-mail

Name

Address

Home Phone   Work Phone

Mobile Phone   E-mail

Name

Address

Home Phone   Work Phone

Mobile Phone   E-mail

Name

Address

Home Phone   Work Phone

Mobile Phone   E-mail

Name

Address

Home Phone   Work Phone

Mobile Phone   E-mail

Name

Address

Home Phone   Work Phone

Mobile Phone   E-mail

Name

Address

Home Phone   Work Phone

Mobile Phone   E-mail

Name

Address

Home Phone   Work Phone

Mobile Phone   E-mail

Name

Address

Home Phone   Work Phone

Mobile Phone   E-mail

Name

Address

Home Phone   Work Phone

Mobile Phone   E-mail

Name

Address

Home Phone   Work Phone

Mobile Phone   E-mail

Name

Address

Home Phone   Work Phone

Mobile Phone   E-mail

Name

Address

Home Phone   Work Phone

Mobile Phone   E-mail

Name

Address

Home Phone   Work Phone

Mobile Phone   E-mail

Name

Address

Home Phone

Work Phone

Mobile Phone

E-mail

Name

Address

Home Phone

Work Phone

Mobile Phone

E-mail

Name

Address

Home Phone

Work Phone

Mobile Phone

E-mail

Name

Address

Home Phone

Work Phone

Mobile Phone

E-mail

Name

Address

Home Phone

Work Phone

Mobile Phone

E-mail

Name

Address

Home Phone   Work Phone

Mobile Phone   E-mail

Name

Address

Home Phone   Work Phone

Mobile Phone   E-mail

Name

Address

Home Phone   Work Phone

Mobile Phone   E-mail

Name

Address

Home Phone   Work Phone

Mobile Phone   E-mail

Name

Address

Home Phone   Work Phone

Mobile Phone   E-mail

Name

Address

Home Phone   Work Phone

Mobile Phone   E-mail

Name

Address

Home Phone   Work Phone

Mobile Phone   E-mail

Name

Address

Home Phone   Work Phone

Mobile Phone   E-mail

Name

Address

Home Phone   Work Phone

Mobile Phone   E-mail

Name

Address

Home Phone   Work Phone

Mobile Phone   E-mail

Name

Address

Home Phone   Work Phone

Mobile Phone   E-mail

Name

Address

Home Phone   Work Phone

Mobile Phone   E-mail

Name

Address

Home Phone   Work Phone

Mobile Phone   E-mail

Name

Address

Home Phone   Work Phone

Mobile Phone   E-mail

Name

Address

Home Phone   Work Phone

Mobile Phone   E-mail

Name

Address

Home Phone   Work Phone

Mobile Phone   E-mail

Name

Address

Home Phone   Work Phone

Mobile Phone   E-mail

Name

Address

Home Phone   Work Phone

Mobile Phone   E-mail

Name

Address

Home Phone   Work Phone

Mobile Phone   E-mail

Name

Address

Home Phone   Work Phone

Mobile Phone   E-mail

Name

Address

Home Phone   Work Phone

Mobile Phone   E-mail

Name

Address

Home Phone   Work Phone

Mobile Phone   E-mail

Name

Address

Home Phone   Work Phone

Mobile Phone   E-mail

Name

Address

Home Phone   Work Phone

Mobile Phone   E-mail

Name

Address

Home Phone   Work Phone

Mobile Phone   E-mail

Name

Address

Home Phone   Work Phone

Mobile Phone   E-mail

Name

Address

Home Phone   Work Phone

Mobile Phone   E-mail

Name

Address

Home Phone   Work Phone

Mobile Phone   E-mail

Name

Address

Home Phone   Work Phone

Mobile Phone   E-mail

Name

Address

Home Phone   Work Phone

Mobile Phone   E-mail

Name

Address

Home Phone   Work Phone

Mobile Phone   E-mail

Name

Address

Home Phone   Work Phone

Mobile Phone   E-mail

Name

Address

Home Phone   Work Phone

Mobile Phone   E-mail

Name

Address

Home Phone   Work Phone

Mobile Phone   E-mail

Name

Address

Home Phone   Work Phone

Mobile Phone   E-mail

Name

Address

Home Phone   Work Phone

Mobile Phone   E-mail

Name

Address

Home Phone   Work Phone

Mobile Phone   E-mail

Name

Address

Home Phone   Work Phone

Mobile Phone   E-mail

Name

Address

Home Phone   Work Phone

Mobile Phone   E-mail

Name

Address

Home Phone   Work Phone

Mobile Phone   E-mail

Name

Address

Home Phone   Work Phone

Mobile Phone   E-mail

Name

Address

Home Phone   Work Phone

Mobile Phone   E-mail

Name

Address

Home Phone   Work Phone

Mobile Phone   E-mail

Name

Address

Home Phone   Work Phone

Mobile Phone   E-mail

Name

Address

Home Phone   Work Phone

Mobile Phone   E-mail

Name

Address

Home Phone   Work Phone

Mobile Phone   E-mail

Name

Address

Home Phone   Work Phone

Mobile Phone   E-mail

Name

Address

Home Phone   Work Phone

Mobile Phone   E-mail

Name

Address

Home Phone   Work Phone

Mobile Phone   E-mail

Name

Address

Home Phone   Work Phone

Mobile Phone   E-mail

Name

Address

Home Phone   Work Phone

Mobile Phone   E-mail

Name

Address

Home Phone   Work Phone

Mobile Phone   E-mail

Name

Address

Home Phone   Work Phone

Mobile Phone   E-mail

Name

Address

Home Phone   Work Phone

Mobile Phone   E-mail

Name

Address

Home Phone   Work Phone

Mobile Phone   E-mail

Name

Address

Home Phone   Work Phone

Mobile Phone   E-mail

Name

Address

Home Phone   Work Phone

Mobile Phone   E-mail

Name

Address

Home Phone   Work Phone

Mobile Phone   E-mail

Name

Address

Home Phone   Work Phone

Mobile Phone   E-mail

Name

Address

Home Phone   Work Phone

Mobile Phone   E-mail

Name _____

Address _____

Home Phone _____ Work Phone _____

Mobile Phone _____ E-mail _____

Name _____

Address _____

Home Phone _____ Work Phone _____

Mobile Phone _____ E-mail _____

Name _____

Address _____

Home Phone _____ Work Phone _____

Mobile Phone _____ E-mail _____

Name _____

Address _____

Home Phone _____ Work Phone _____

Mobile Phone _____ E-mail _____

Name _____

Address _____

Home Phone _____ Work Phone _____

Mobile Phone _____ E-mail _____

Name

Address

Home Phone   Work Phone

Mobile Phone   E-mail

Name

Address

Home Phone   Work Phone

Mobile Phone   E-mail

Name

Address

Home Phone   Work Phone

Mobile Phone   E-mail

Name

Address

Home Phone   Work Phone

Mobile Phone   E-mail

Name

Address

Home Phone   Work Phone

Mobile Phone   E-mail

Name

Address

Home Phone   Work Phone

Mobile Phone   E-mail

Name

Address

Home Phone   Work Phone

Mobile Phone   E-mail

Name

Address

Home Phone   Work Phone

Mobile Phone   E-mail

Name

Address

Home Phone   Work Phone

Mobile Phone   E-mail

Name

Address

Home Phone   Work Phone

Mobile Phone   E-mail

Name

Address

Home Phone   Work Phone

Mobile Phone   E-mail

Name

Address

Home Phone   Work Phone

Mobile Phone   E-mail

Name

Address

Home Phone   Work Phone

Mobile Phone   E-mail

Name

Address

Home Phone   Work Phone

Mobile Phone   E-mail

Name

Address

Home Phone   Work Phone

Mobile Phone   E-mail

Name

Address

Home Phone   Work Phone

Mobile Phone   E-mail

Name

Address

Home Phone   Work Phone

Mobile Phone   E-mail

Name

Address

Home Phone   Work Phone

Mobile Phone   E-mail

Name

Address

Home Phone   Work Phone

Mobile Phone   E-mail

Name

Address

Home Phone   Work Phone

Mobile Phone   E-mail

Funeral Arrangements

Funeral Home Selection

Death Notice/Obituary

Public or Private Funeral

Casket Selection

Special Flowers

Burial Plot

Special Pallbearers

Headstone or Monument Selection & Inscription

Memorial Contributions

Desired Clothing

Cosmetology

Meaningful Mementos

Post-Funeral Reception

"Death leaves a heartache no one can heal.
Life leaves a memory no one can steal."
~Anonymous

Funeral Arrangements

When a loved one dies, grieving family members and friends are often confronted with many difficult decisions about the funeral – most of which must be made quickly and often under great emotional duress. Planning ahead will not only allow you to make informed and thoughtful decisions regarding the funeral arrangements, but will save your loved ones from additional stress.

Use this segment of your journal as a guide to help express your personal wishes pertaining to your funeral arrangements. It is important to note that these preferences should not be designated only in your will, since a will often is not found or read until after the funeral. Also avoid placing the only copy of your wishes in a safety deposit box. Your family may have to make arrangements on a weekend or holiday, before the safety deposit box can be opened.

Funeral Home Selection

Address

Telephone

Death Notice/Obituary

Newspaper Selections

Public or Private

Pre-Paid Funeral Contracts   ☐ Yes   ☐ No

Location of Documents

Casket Selection

Special Flowers

Cemetery Selection

Location

Burial Plot

Potential Pallbearers

Name
_____

Telephone
_____

Name
_____

Telephone
_____

Name
_____

Telephone
_____

Name
_____

Telephone
_____

Name
_____

Telephone
_____

Name
_____

Telephone
_____

Name
_____

Telephone
_____

Headstone or Monument Selection & Inscription

Company Name

Address

Telephone

Inscription

Memorial Contributions (Favorite Charities, Organizations)

Desired Clothing

_____

_____

_____

_____

Desired Jewelry

_____

_____

_____

_____

Cosmetology (hairstyle and make-up)

Salon Name

Favorite Stylist

Salon Address

Telephone

(See enclosed photo)

Additional Comments

_____

_____

_____

_____

Meaningful Mementos to be Placed with the Body

Post-Funeral Reception

Name

Location

Special Wishes

Additional Comments

The Dash

I read of a man who stood to speak
at the funeral of a friend.
He referred to the dates on her tombstone
from the beginning... to the end.

He noted that first came the date of her birth
and spoke the following date with tears,
but he said what mattered most of all
was the dash between those years.

For that dash represents all the time
that she spent alive on earth
and now only those who loved her
know what that little line is worth.

For it matters not how much we own,
the cars... the house... the cash.
What matters is how we live and love
and how we spend our dash.

So think about this long and hard,
are there things you'd like to change?
For you never know how much time is left
that can still be rearranged.

If we could just slow down enough
to consider what's true and real
and always try to understand
the way other people feel.

And be less quick to anger
and show appreciation more
and love the people in our lives
like we've never loved before.

If we treat each other with respect
and more often wear a smile
remembering that this special dash
might only last a little while.

So when your eulogy is being read
with your life's actions to rehash,
would you be proud of the things they say
about how you spent your dash?

Religious Wishes

Place of Worship

Special Clergy

Personal Eulogy

Desired Speakers at the Service

Favorite Music

Favorite Readings

Favorite Poems

God will always take care of you...
"For He has said, 'I will never leave you or forsake you.'"
~ Hebrews 13:5 (NRSV)

Religious Wishes

Most funerals in our culture are based on religion. Even though they are largely similar, there are differences among them. The traditional funeral may be changing, but its purpose has not. A funeral is still an important ceremony that provides needed support to the bereaved.

If you would like to personalize your religious service, use this segment of your journal to express those wishes to your loved ones.

Religious Wishes

Place of Worship

Church, Synagogue, Mosque, or Other Public Facility

Special Clergy

Personal Eulogy

"God may not always be obvious, but He is there:
discernible, knowable, reachable, dependable, and ever welcoming."

-Anonymous

Desired Speakers at the Service

Favorite Music (songs and hymns)

Special Vocalist

Special Musicians

List of Favorite Readings

List of Favorite Poems

"Those who can find no reason for giving thanks-
Never start,
While those who understand, know no reason-
To ever stop."
-Anonymous

Additional Wishes

Serenity Prayer

God grant me the serenity
to accept the things
I cannot change,
the courage to change
the things I can,
and the wisdom
to know the difference.

~ Reinhold Niebuhr

Cremation

Authorization Forms
Funeral Home and Cremation Services
Disposition of Cremated Remains
Memorial Service

"The way you leave this life
may be as unique and personal as the way you live it."
~Anonymous

Cremation

While different cultures and religions have their own distinctive customs, funeral and cremation services all share a common goal – to honor the person who died and bring closure to family and friends.

With a little guidance and a great deal of support, a well-planned, thoughtful cremation service can be a very comforting way to honor the life of a loved one.

Use this segment of your journal to indicate your wishes for cremation to your loved ones.

Cremation Authorization Forms

Location of Documents

Funeral Home and Cremation Services

Special Location to Place Cremated Remains

Memorial Service

Location

Special Wishes

An Irish Blessing

May the road rise to meet you,
May the winds always be at your back,
May the sun shine warm on your face,
The rains fall soft upon your fields,
And until we meet again,
May God hold you in the hollow of His hand.

Legal and Financial

Wills and Trusts

Insurance Policies

Accounting

Financial Institutions

Investments

Credit Cards

Property Deeds

Mortgage Papers

Leases

Motor Vehicle Titles

Other Important Documents and Information

Safety Deposit Box

"Health is the greatest gift,
contentment the greatest wealth,
faithfulness the best relationship."
~ Anonymous

Legal and Financial

The following pages of your journal are designed to assist you and your loved ones in identifying and locating important information pertaining to legal and financial matters.

Avoid placing the only copy of your wishes in a safety deposit box. Your family may have to make arrangements on a weekend or holiday, before the safety deposit box can be opened.

Wills and Trusts

Attorney Name

Address

Telephone   E-mail

Location of Documents

Insurance Policies

Company Name

Insurance Agent

Address

Telephone   E-mail

Username   Password

Location of Insurance Policies

Accounting

Company Name

Accountant Name

Address

Telephone   E-mail

Financial Institutions

Bank Name

Address

Telephone   E-mail

Account Type   Account Number

Bank Name

Address

Telephone   E-mail

Account Type   Account Number

Bank Name

Address

Telephone   E-mail

Account Type   Account Number

Bank Name

Address

Telephone   E-mail

Account Type   Account Number

Investments (Stocks and Bonds)

Brokerage House
_____

Financial Advisor or Stockbroker
_____

Address
_____

Telephone   Account Number
_____

Username   Password
_____

Brokerage House
_____

Financial Advisor or Stockbroker
_____

Address
_____

Telephone   Account Number
_____

Username   Password
_____

Credit Cards

Credit Card Name
_____

Account Number
_____

Telephone
_____

Credit Card Name
_____

Account Number
_____

Telephone
_____

Credit Card Name

Account Number

Telephone

Credit Card Name

Account Number

Telephone

Credit Card Name

Account Number

Telephone

Credit Card Name

Account Number

Telephone

Credit Card Name

Account Number

Telephone

Property Deeds

Type of Property
_____

Name of Mortgage Lender
_____

Location of Deed
_____

Mortgage Account Number
_____

Telephone
_____

Username _____ Password _____

Type of Property
_____

Name of Mortgage Lender
_____

Location of Deed
_____

Mortgage Account Number
_____

Telephone
_____

Username _____ Password _____

Type of Property
_____

Name of Mortgage Lender
_____

Location of Deed
_____

Mortgage Account Number
_____

Telephone
_____

Username _____ Password _____

Mortgage Papers

_____

_____

_____

Location of Documents

_____

Motor Vehicle Titles

_____

Location of Documents

_____

Others (boats, airplanes, etc.)

_____

Location of Documents

_____

Contracts (auto leases, etc.)

_____

_____

Location of Documents

_____

Other Important Documents and Information

Birth Certificate
_____

Location of Document
_____

Social Security Number and Records
_____

Location of Documents
_____

Citizenship Papers
_____

Location of Documents
_____

Divorce Papers
_____

Location of Documents
_____

Medicare Documents
_____

Location of Documents
_____

Pension and Retirement Benefits Information
_____

Location of Documents
_____

Safety Deposit Box ☐ Yes ☐ No

Location of Safety Deposit Box
_____

_____

Person(s) authorized to access safety deposit box

Name _____

Relationship _____

Telephone _____

Name _____

Relationship _____

Telephone _____

Location of Lists of Personal Identification Numbers (PINs), Combinations and Passwords to Any Protected Information

_____

_____

_____

_____

_____

_____

Additional Comments

Special Care

Minor Children

Dependent Adults

"The best and most beautiful things in the world
cannot be seen or touched...
they must be felt with the heart."
~ Helen Keller

Special Care of Minor Children and Dependent Adults

Determining guardianship for your children or a dependent adult is one of the most serious decisions you can make. It is an issue which should be discussed and managed with qualified professional assistance.

This segment of your journal may assist you in clarifying this important matter.

Care of Minor Children

Names of Children
_____

_____

_____

_____

_____

Name of Guardian
_____

Address
_____

Telephone
_____

Location of Guardianship Documents
_____

_____

Additional Comments
_____

_____

_____

_____

_____

_____

_____

_____

Whispers of a Child's Love

A child's love is like a whisper,
given in little ways we do not hear.
But if you listen closely,
it will be very clear.

They often do not say it loud,
but in how they come to you...
Daddy, will you play with me?
Mommy, tie my shoe?

The many ways they tell you
changes as they grow...
Dad, I made the team today!
Mom, I've got to go!

Pop, I need some money
You see there's this girl at school...
Mama, I met a boy today
and wow, he is so cool!

Dad, I've got something to tell you...
I think she is the one.
Mom, he asked me to marry him.
Would you love him as your son?

Dad, I've got some news for you...
It's gonna be a boy!
Mom, I'm kind of scared of this,
yet I'm filled with joy!

A child's love is like a whisper,
given in little ways we do not hear.
But if you listen closely
it will be very clear.

They often do not say it loud,
but in how they come to you...
Grandpa, will you play with me?
Grandma, tie my shoe...

It is never ending,
A blessing from above.
Listen to the whispers
of a child's love.

S.E. Chan, copyright 1999

Care of Dependent Adults

Names of Dependent Adults
_____

_____

_____

_____

_____

Name of Caregiver
_____

Address
_____

Telephone
_____

Location of Guardianship Documents
_____

_____

_____

Additional Comments
_____

_____

_____

_____

_____

_____

_____

_____

About Promises

Promises
Should be
Taken seriously
Because
They involve
Something
That will
Somehow
Touch
The future
Of some life.

Special Care
of Pets

"A dog is the only thing on earth
that loves you more than you love yourself."
~ Josh Billings (1818-1885)

Special Care of Pets

Pets can play a very important role in our lives. They become part of our cherished memories through the years. They have been there in times of happiness and times of sorrow. Pets offer us unconditional love, while being dependent upon us for the basic necessities of life. Pets are loyal companions and are considered to be part of the family.

Use this segment of your journal to make certain your special pet continues to receive the loving care that you have always provided.

My Pets

Type of Pets and Names

_____

_____

_____

_____

Age of Pets

_____

Breed of Pets

_____

_____

Breeder's Name

_____

Address

_____

Telephone

_____

Veterinarian's Name

_____

Address

_____

Telephone

_____

Veterinarian's Name

_____

Address

_____

Telephone

_____

Kennel Name
_____

Address
_____

Telephone
_____

Groomer's Name
_____

Address
_____

Telephone
_____

Future Caretaker
_____

Address
_____

Telephone
_____

Future Caretaker
_____

Address
_____

Telephone
_____

Feeding Requirements/Schedule (type of food, frequency and quantity)

_____

_____

_____

_____

Vitamin and/or Medication Schedule (names and dosages)

_____

_____

_____

_____

Favorite Toys and Treats

_____

_____

_____

Exercise Schedule

_____

Location of Important Documents (vaccination records, medical records, dental records, pedigree information, etc.)

_____

_____

_____

_____

Additional Comments

_____

_____

_____

Pet Quotes

"Women and cats will do as they please,
and men and dogs should relax and get used to the idea."

~ Robert A. Heinlein

"In order to keep a true perspective of one's importance,
everyone should have a dog that will worship him
and a cat that will ignore him."

~ Dereke Bruce, Taipei, Taiwan

"Dogs come when they're called;
cats take a message and get back to you later."

~ Mary Bly

"You can say any fool thing to a dog,
and the dog will give you this look that says,
My Gosh, you're right! I NEVER would've thought of that!"

~ Dave Barry, US Columnist & Humorist

"If you pick up a starving dog and make him prosperous,
he will not bite you; that is the principal difference
between a dog and a man."

~ Mark Twain

"Don't accept your dog's admiration
as conclusive evidence that you are wonderful."

~ Ann Landers

Wellness Tips We Can Learn from A Dog

Never pass up the opportunity to go for a joy ride.
Let the experience of fresh air in your face be pure ecstasy.
When loved ones come home, always run to greet them.
Let others know when they've invaded your territory.
When it's in your best interest, practice obedience.
Take naps and stretch before rising.
Run, romp and play daily.
Eat with gusto and enthusiasm.
Be loyal.
Never pretend to be something you're not.
If what you want lies buried, dig until you find it.
When someone is having a bad day, be silent, sit close by
and nuzzle them gently.
Avoid biting when a simple growl will do.
On hot days, drink lots of water and lay under a shady tree.
When you're happy, dance around and wag your entire body.
If you're scolded, don't buy into the guilt thing.
Run right back and make friends.
Delight in the simple joy of a long walk.

Special Memories

Family

Friends

Occasions

"My family and friends have made
the story of my life."
~Anonymous

Special Memories

There are times in one's life that are notable in strengthening relationships and celebrating the joy of sharing love and life with others. These special times include, birthdays, anniversaries, holidays, graduations, reunions, travels and accomplishments.

Your recollections in this segment of your journal will be cherished by your loved ones and provide an everlasting source of loving memories.

"Today is mine - a gift to be opened, a path waiting to be taken, an empty page for me to fill with my own meaning."

~Anonymous

Family Ties

Family ties are precious things
Woven through the years
of laughter, love and tears.

Family ties are cherished things
forged in childhood days,
by love of parents deep and true,
by traditions, by family ways.

Family ties are treasured things
and far though we may roam,
the tender bond with those we love
still pull our hearts toward home.

~ Virginia Blanck Moore

Special Memories of Family

"*Favorite people, favorite places,
favorite memories of the past...
These are the joys of a lifetime,
these are the things that last.*"

~Anonymous

"The beauty of
the written word is that
it can be held
close to the heart and read
over and over again."

~ Florence Littauer

Special Memories of Friends

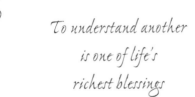

To understand another
is one of life's
richest blessings

and to be understood
by another
is perhaps love's sweetest,
most satisfying
gift.

~ Ernest Hemingway

"Don't cry because it is over,
       Smile because it happened."
                              ~Anonymous

"Life is not measured
       by the number of breaths we take,
but by the moments
       that take our breath away."
                              ~Anonymous

Memories of Special Occasions

Memories Yet To Be

Life - a gift that at times
Seems to lose its rhyme
With its moments moving fast, yet slow.
Sometimes seems to lose its glow.

But after the thunder of the evening storm
And the morning's sunlight beginning to be born,
Yields a brighter day with a gentle breeze.
A new beginning, a broken heart freed.

A bird, a flower, a lover's embrace,
A day with smiles, a child's face,
A heart that stirs, that longs to see.
My soul content with memories yet to be.

- Robert Krumroy

Special
Written
Messages

Family

Friends

"Write it on your heart
that everyday is the best day of the year."
- Ralph Waldo Emerson

Special Written Messages

A personal written message is one of the most intimate ways to communicate with a loved one. Verbally expressing our true thoughts and feelings to someone is often postponed or left undone.

You are likely to experience many emotions as you recollect aspects of your life. You may need to ask others to forgive you. Or you may need to forgive those who have hurt or disappointed you. There may be people who have played a significant role in your life to whom you would like to offer thanks and express your appreciation.

Use this segment of your journal to encourage your inner voice to speak. Acknowledging your imperfections and those of others can be very meaningful and provide comfort and peace of mind.

Special Written Messages to my Family

Friendship's Tapestry

So often when I think of you and all the times we shared,
My heart is filled with thankfulness to have a friend who cared
enough to listen to me tell of joys and trials.
Your being there has been enough to change my tears to smiles.

The subtle love between two friends is so hard to define.
It is not a square or circle or even a straight line.
It's somehow like a tapestry with colors soft and bold,
yet deep within the weaving there are tiny threads of gold.

Yes, rare and oh so lovely are your friendships' threads of gold,
For they will last a lifetime, and then when my story's told,
Someone will hold my tapestry and turn it towards the light
and tiny points, those threads of gold will gleam and shine so bright.
And they may think – it's just a thread like green or red or blue –
Perhaps they'll never ever know that golden thread was you.

But I've been thinking lately how you've touched my life just so.
Of how you are so dear to me – and I wanted you to know –
That even if you're next to me, or though we're miles apart
Your golden thread of friendship still will weave within my heart.

Special
Written
Messages
to my
Friends

My Favorite Photographs

My Favorite Photographs

Loving memories are keepsakes of the heart.
Use these journal pages to display your favorite
photographs and mementos.

Build a lifetime of memories for your loved ones,
recording important names, dates and occasions
in the "Special Comments" area.

Special Comments

Special Comments

Special Comments

Special Comments

Give them peace of mind.
Give them a sense of history.
Give them "Grant Me My Final Wish."

You've taken the step toward providing more emotional security for you and your loved ones. Now you can provide that guidance for someone else.

Grant Me My Final Wish is more than a guide. It's your legacy, a family history that can be shared for generations. Now you can order additional copies of this journal for family and friends and show them how to give the greatest gift of all – yourself.

CHECK YOUR LOCAL BOOKSTORE OR ORDER HERE.
Volume discounts are available by contacting the publisher, Bella Vita Books at 1-800-589-0039 or www.bellavitabooks.com.

☐ YES, I want _____ copies of *Grant Me My Final Wish* at $24.95 each plus $5 shipping per book (Michigan residents, please add $1.49 sales tax per book). Canadian orders must be accompanied by a postal money order in US funds. Allow 15 days for delivery.

☐ My check or money order for $ _____ is enclosed.
☐ Please charge my: ___Visa ___MasterCard ___Discover ___American Express

Name _____

Organization _____

Address _____

City/State/Zip _____

Phone _____ E-mail _____

Credit Card # _____

Exp. Date _____ Signature _____

Please make check payable and return to:
Bella Vita Books, LLC
1265 Water Cliff Drive
Bloomfield Hills, MI 48302

Credit card orders by mail, by phone (1-800-589-0039),
or online at: www.bellavitabooks.com

Final Wish

When I climb the stairway to Heaven
I know what will await me at the top,
It will be a sight so beautiful
that it will almost make my heart stop.
A light so bright
will shine into my eyes,
There will finally be answers
to all of my many "Whys."
As I look around
I know that I will see,
My Saviour will be there
with open arms to welcome me.
My final wish will be granted
as He says, "Come and you will see,"
My heart filled with utter joy
as He gives you back to me!

Some People

Some people come into our lives and quickly go.
Some people move our souls to dance.
They awaken us to new understanding,
With the passing whisper of their wisdom.

Some people make the sky more beautiful to gaze upon.
They stay in our lives for awhile,
Leave footprints on our hearts,
And we are never, ever, the same.

Anonymous